PROPERTY OF
This Kinky Mofo

....

Table of Contents

Me BDSM & Kink...

This section explores the kinky side of who you are and how to go deeper into that discovery and exploration.

Oh Memories

This section goes over the play by plays of your goals, best, and worst version of your kink journey.

Playtime

This section goes over all the important components to understand before, during and after playtime!

Extras

Extra Journal Pages and more!

What's Up Kinky Peeps

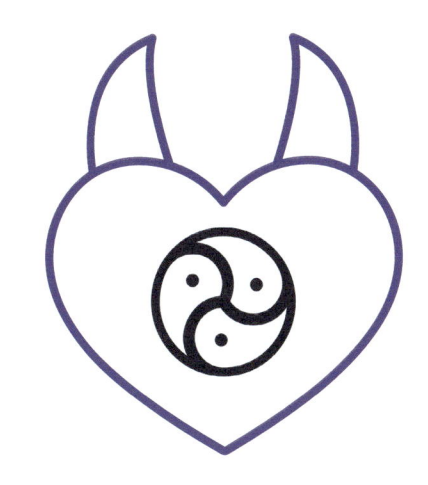

I'm so excited to see you exploring that secret forbidden part of you! It takes a lot of courage, strength, and challenging work to be your best kinky self! To help you along the way, I've curated this workbook & Journal to assist you in diving deeper and exploring just how kinky you can be. Though this working journal is meant to be used in conjunction with my BDSM 101 Book, This journal is easy enough to work with on its own as well. Do note that If something is unfamiliar to you, peep the resource page on my site kinkinkolor.com to help lead you towards the answers you're looking or you can also use the interwebs;)

It is perfectly fine to move at your own pace; in fact, I encourage you to not rush the process. While this journal does give you a strong foundation on what to look for and how to go about it, remember this journal is to help you identify what works best for you. Some of these tools may work better than others, some may not work as you expect or some may not work at all. A lot of these things that are listed here are intended to keep you as safe as possible while doing all the kinky ish you've wanted to do. If you don't do it this way it doesn't mean you're wrong, just don't knock it, till you've tried it yeah?

Also, the use of the word partner does not necessarily mean that this is someone that you are romantically involved with, this can also mean someone that you are platonically, sexually, online, or casually involved with. It's also set up to be as gender-neutral as possible since we all have different gender/sexual expressions, and identities.

Last but not least, be honest with yourself and where you are right now. Your thoughts and feelings can change over time and as you grow, learn and gain more experience it will only change more. Don't compare your journey to someone else's and just enjoy the ride. Have fun and remember, at this moment, right now you are in control, you are present, and you are doing your best!

ME
BDSM
AND KINK...

WHAT DOES BDSM & KINK MEAN TO ME?

WAYS I'D LIKE TO EXPLORE KINK

Code Of Ethics

Write the pros & cons of each code and create your own

SSC

RACK

PRICK

MY OWN

Different Dynamics

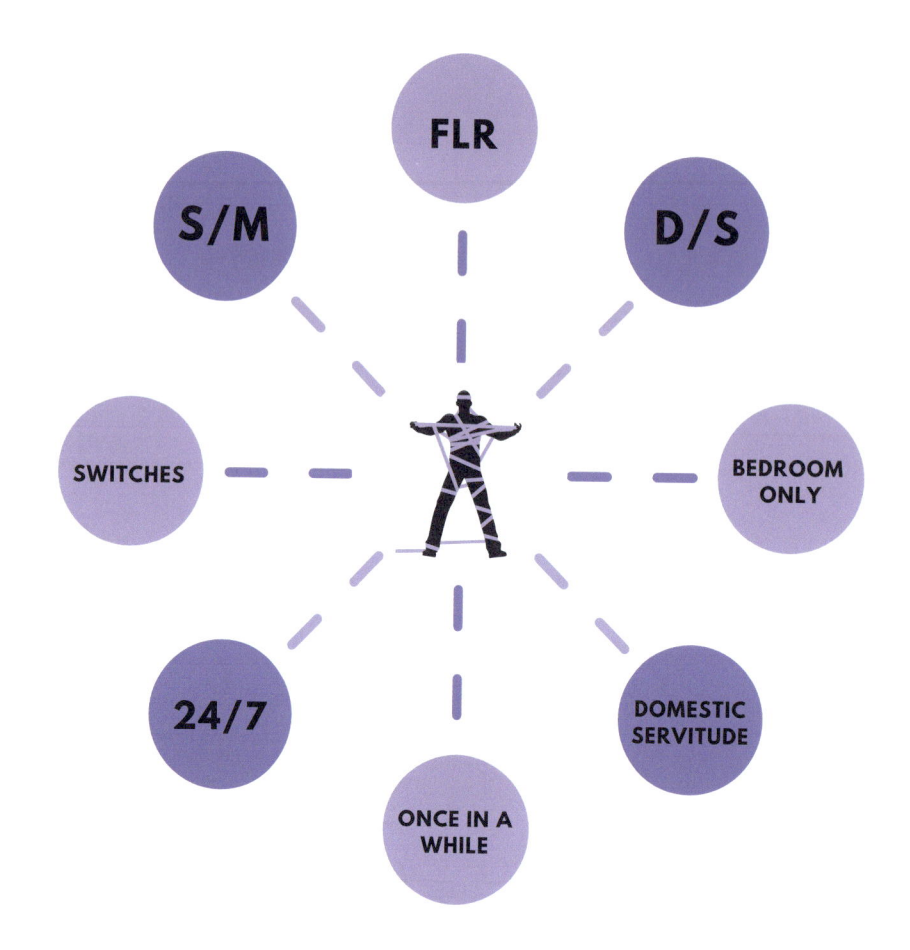

- FLR
- D/S
- S/M
- BEDROOM ONLY
- SWITCHES
- DOMESTIC SERVITUDE
- 24/7
- ONCE IN A WHILE

Use the ideas above to figure out what your kinky or BDSM dynamic will be.

Name: _____   Date: _____

Understanding

Write your list of kinks and see where you fall. Are you more one than the other, a combo of it all, or pretty vanilla with a bit of spice?

Fetishest	Kinkster
BDSM Player	My Own

I'm innocent until proven naughty

Yes! No. Maybe? List

KEY
- Yes: Love, Like, Want
- Nah: Not into it at all
- M?: Maybe, Open just not now
- 0-5: Experience Level

This isn't an exhaustive list, but these are the most common things you'll come across.
*Note: This is created to be as Gender & Sexually neutral as possible including Poly & LGBTQI+ dynamics.

Basics | Yes | Nah | M? | 0-5
- Anal Play
- Anal Sex
- Biting
- Blowjobs
- Breeding
- Creampie
- Cuddling
- Cunnilingus
- Cupping
- Deep Throat
- Dirty Talk
- Double Penetration
- Edging
- Face-Fucking
- Face-Sitting
- Facials
- Fingering
- G-Spot
- Hand jobs
- P-Spot
- PDA
- Pegging
- Rimming
- Rough Sex
- Scratching
- SexToys (vibrator, plug, etc)
- Sixty Nine (69)
- Swallowing
- Teasing
- Watching Porn
- Worship (Pussy, Cock, Ass)

Group Things | Yes | Nah | M?
- BiCuriosity /Hetero/ Homo Flexibility
- Gangbang
- MF
- MFF
- MM
- MMF
- ONS
- Orgy
- Queer Coupling
- Swinger
- Bull
- Cuck

Relationship | Yes | Nah | M?
- Casual
- Ethically Non-Monogamous (ENM)
- FWB
- Kitchen Table Poly
- Mono-Poly
- Monogam-ish
- Monogamous
- Open Relationship
- Parallel Poly
- Poly Amorous
- Poly Fidelity
- Relationship Anarchy
- Solo Poly
- Triad/Throuple
- Unicorn

Kinky/Fetish Play | Yes | Nah | M? | 0-5
- Blindfolds
- Body Worship
- Bondage (Shibari, Kinbaku..etc)
- Boot Worship
- Bootblacking
- Choking (Light)
- Clothespins
- Cock Rings
- Collar/Leash
- Cross Dressing
- Cuffs
- Erotic Massage
- Erotic Wrestling
- Exhibitionism
- Face Slapping
- Fisting
- Food Play
- Foot Worship
- Forced Orgasm
- Frottage
- Furry
- Hair Pulling
- Hedonist
- Human Ashtray
- JOI Instructions
- Latex, Leather Worship
- Making Videos
- Mutual Masturbation
- Oils & Lotions
- Phone Sex
- Pregnant
- Public Sex
- Sensation Play
- Sensory Deprivation
- Showers (red, brown, roman)
- Spanking (Light)
- Swinging
- Tantra
- Tease & Denial
- Tickling
- Voyeur
- Watersports
- Waxplay

AfterCare | Yes | Nah | M?
- Candy
- Comfortable Silence
- Conversation
- Cuddles
- Sex
- Solitude

BDSM | Yes | Nah | M? | 0-5
- Age Play
- Blackmail
- Bondage (Hard)
- Bottom
- Breath Play
- CBT
- CFNM
- Chastity
- CMNF
- Consent Non Consent
- Daddy
- Degradation
- Disciplinarian
- Doll
- Dominant
- Estim
- Femdom
- Findom
- Flogging
- Gags
- Heavy Masochist
- Hig Protocol
- Human Furniture
- Human Toilet
- Humiliation
- Impact Play
- Marks
- Masochist
- Master
- Medical Play
- MindFuck
- Mommy
- Mummification
- Nipple Clamps
- Online Domination
- Orgasm Denial
- Pet
- Pony Play
- Power Exchange
- Pro Dom/Domme
- Pro Sub
- Resistance Play
- Ritual
- Sadist
- Sensual
- Sissification/Feminization
- Slave
- Sounding
- Spanko
- Submissive
- Switch
- Top
- Trampling
- Water Bondage

(BDSM) EDGE Play | Yes | Nah | M? | 0-5
- (Bondage) Suspension
- Branding
- Bulwhip
- Cell Popping
- Cutting
- Electric Play
- Encasement
- Fire Play
- Knife Play
- Needle Play
- Singletail
- Staples

WHAT ARE THE KINKY THINGS I LIKE?

WHAT ARE MY SOFT & HARD LIMITS?

Introspective

These are other things you should identify before jumping into play/scenes/or kink fun

TRIGGERS?

MEDICAL PRECAUTIONS?

AFTERCARE

CREATE YOUR OWN

SAFETY PROTOCOL
WHAT DO I NEED TO FEEL SAFE BEFORE, AFTER & DURING A KINKY TIME?

Ex: Having a safe person to call, having security, using an app, etc.

SafeWords:
- All Good:
- Let's Pause For a Sec:
- Stop That's Too Far:

SafeGestures:
- All Good:
- Let's Pause For a Sec:
- Stop That's Too Far:

Safety Apps:

SafeCall Person:

WHAT ARE SOME RED FLAGS I NOTICE IN POTENTIAL PARTNERS?

EXAMPLE: USING BDSM TERMS TOO EARLY, NOT NEGOTIATING BEFORE TRYING SOMETHING NEW...ETC

HOW DO I FEEL ABOUT PLAY CENTERED AROUND RACE/POLITICS...ETC?

MY SKILLZ

What kinks are you good at? Are there any you want to learn? It's ok if you don't have many, we all have to start somewhere!

Toy & Gear List

LET'S SEE WHAT KINKY-ISH YOU ALREADY HAVE!

Gear

_____
_____
_____
_____
_____
_____
_____

Sexual Toys

_____
_____
_____
_____
_____
_____
_____

Non Sexual Toys

_____
_____
_____
_____
_____
_____
_____

Pervertables

_____
_____
_____
_____
_____
_____
_____

PLAYTIME 😈

Don't *tease* me if you aren't going to *Please Me.*

HOW TO VET PLAY PARTNERS

It's always important to vet potential partners and/or play/scene partners before you get to the fun stuff. Here are some ideas & questions that can help you form your own process.

- Check out any of the profiles they have online, whether it's Dating, Socials, or something similar to FetLife.
- If you met through a friend (or through the local kink community), ask their opinion but take what you hear with a grain of salt.
- Does your vanilla stuff match up?
- Do your Kinks match up?
- Do they have any <u>real-life</u> experience doing what they do?
- How will you keep each other safe?

Create Your Own

Negotiation

THINGS TO DISCUSS BEFORE PLAYING WITH YOUR PARTNER

My Partner likes To Be Called:

My Partner identifies as?

Date & Duration of play:

Where will we play?

What are my Partner's interests & likes?

Main things we want to explore for our scene: (start with 2-3)

Is there chemistry? Y/N
What are their limits?

Any Mental Health, Medical Challenges, or Triggers to look out for?

How will I keep my Partner safe?

What does my Partner need for aftercare?

Will sex/drugs/alcohol be involved? How?

THE DIFFERENTLY ABLED

Sometimes your partner may have a physical or mental uniqueness that makes you think a bit more outside the box (e.g. wheelchair... etc). Discuss these prompts with your partner to see what works best.

HELPFUL RESOURCES

FEARS I HAVE

CREATIVE WAYS TO USE FURNITURE

REMINDERS

NOTES

KINKY PARENTS
Cheat Sheet

DATE: ....

PLACES TO HIDE TOYS

1. ....
2. ....
3. ....

Non Verbal Power Exchange ideas

THE KIDS HEARD/SAW...WHAT TO DO?

CODE WORDS:

NEXT KINKY DATE NIGHT:

OUR RULES/GUIDELINES

Will there be rules or guidelines involved? If so, use this page as a to create your own rules/guidelines for the dynamic you wish to have!

NAUGHTY PLAYLIST

All good fun has a sexy playlist! Write down the songs that get you in that naughty, kinky, power exchanging headspace!

THINK OF OTHER WAYS TO GET YOURSELF AND/OR YOUR PARTNER IN THE ZONE

PLAYTIME
Inspiration

What ideas, thoughts, and protocols will be used for our kinkyfun?

ROLEPLAY
Ideas

Let your fantasy run wild! Think of the costumes you have, Where you'd like to play, or What characters you'd have fun playing!

My *kinky* preference is...OFTEN.

Fun words to use/hear in scene

Here are a few words to get you started:

Slut	**Bitchboy**		

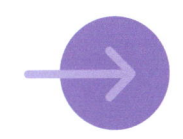

After our scene...

Instruction

write down a brief rundown of how your scene went.

MY FAVORITE

Toys we tried
- ....
- ....
- ....
- ....
- ....
- ....

I learned :

WHAT WENT WELL?

....
....
....
....

WHAT WENT NOT AS WELL?

....
....
....
....

FAVORITE THING THAT HAPPENED:

WRITE OUT YOUR LONGER THOUGHTS AND FEELINGS ABOUT HOW IT WENT.

WHAT TO DO DURING Sub-Drop

Create a Sub-Drop Intervention Protocol.

WHAT TO DO DURING *Top-Drop*

Create a Top-Drop Intervention Protocol.

OTHER WAYS TO *Play*

ONLINE ONLY? LET'S GET THAT PROFILE RIGHT

Important Things

Top Interests/Hobbies:

1.
2.
3.
4.

Kinks I'm looking for?

1.
2.
3.
4.

What Do I Have to Offer?

1.
2.
3.
4.

Ways I'm proactively learning on my own:

Adjectives that describes me

Dealbreakers

First things others notice

Online BDSM
Starter sheet (tailor it to you)

DATE:

TASKS GIVEN

-
-
-
-
-
-

PLAY DATES

REWARDS

PUNISHMENTS

-
-
-
-
-
-

CREATING A RITUAL

Want to add a little extra to your playtime, creating a ritual is another way to put you & your partner in the right headspace!

A few ideas to get things going	Examples

Create your environment.

1.
2.
3.
4.

Sacred Room, Space, or Greeting

How do you want to be greeted?

1.
2.
3.
4.

Kneeling, Text, or Collaring

Punishments/Rewards

1.
2.
3.
4.

Things they like/dislike

Check In? Is it working?

| List 3 acceptable punishments | List any non-acceptable punishments | Other concerns? |

PUNISHMENT

If this is a part of your M/s or D/s dynamic, use these boxes to describe punishments, rewards, and funishment that is acceptable for you and your play partners. Make sure that the punishments/rewards fits the deed and makes sense for your partner.

REWARD

| List 3 Rewards you'd like to receive. | Big rewards or small ones? | What are you favorite types of rewards? |

List your favorite types of FUNISHMENT:)

OH
Memories

MY FAVE KINK SCENES

Who: **Date:**

Where: **Length:**

Toys/Gears used:

Best Part:

Lessons Learned?

Things to remember for next time:

Would I play with this partner again? Why?

MY FAVE KINK SCENES

Who: **Date:**

Where: **Length:**

Toys/Gears used:

Best Part:

Lessons Learned?

Things to remember for next time:

Would I play with this partner again? Why?

MY FAVE KINK SCENES

Who: **Date:**

Where: **Length:**

Toys/Gears used:

Best Part:

Lessons Learned?

Things to remember for next time:

Would I play with this partner again? Why?

MY WORST KINK SCENES

Who:
Where:

Date:
Length:

Toys/Gears used:

Worst Part & Why:

Lessons Learned?

How do I feel? Should I talk to someone about it?

Would I play with this partner again? Why?

BDSM IS NOT ABUSE

Because a lot of movies and books get this wrong....

Even if you're about that CNC life...it's still negotiated and consented to before engagement.

- A form of consensual power exchange where all participants are empowered.
- Has rules, limits, and boundaries that must be respected at all times (usually discussed during negotiation **before** play).
- There are safety measures in place and a general code of conduct most members of the community ascribe to.
- There is open communication and a safe space for all parties involved to voice opinions, thoughts, emotions, grievances, and ideas.
- It can be fun, cathartic, therapeutic, or sexy,

    In short, a good time for everyone involved!

BDSM is not an excuse to be abusive (emotionally, physically, or mentally)

Abuse takes away another person's power.

- BDSM should not cause anyone to fear and/or be afraid of their partner.
- BDSM should not become a one-sided dynamic without proper negotiation, consent, or safety protocols in place.
- BDSM is not used as a way to intentionally take their anger, hurt, or insecurities out on their partners.
- BDSM is not a place to take what you want, physically, emotionally, and/or mentally.

    For more resources on this subject, check out kinkinkolor.com

Kinky Goals for the Year

JANUARY	FEBRUARY

MARCH	APRIL

MAY	JUNE

JULY	AUGUST

SEPTEMBER	OCTOBER

NOVEMBER	DECEMBER

Goal:

Start: End:

ACTION STEPS

MILESTONES

SUMMARY

-
-
-
-
-
-
-
-

YOU'VE REACHED THE END OF THE WORKBOOK (YAY)...NOW USE THESE NEXT PAGES FOR JOURNALING, NOTES, EXTRAS, OR WHATEVS!

MY THOUGHTS

MY THOUGHTS

MY THOUGHTS

MY THOUGHTS

MY THOUGHTS

MY THOUGHTS

MY THOUGHTS

MY THOUGHTS

MY THOUGHTS

MY THOUGHTS

MY THOUGHTS

MY THOUGHTS

MY THOUGHTS

MY THOUGHTS

MY THOUGHTS

MY THOUGHTS

MY THOUGHTS

MY THOUGHTS

MY THOUGHTS

MY THOUGHTS

MY THOUGHTS

MY THOUGHTS

MY THOUGHTS

MY THOUGHTS

MY THOUGHTS

MY THOUGHTS

MY THOUGHTS

MY THOUGHTS

MY THOUGHTS

MY THOUGHTS

MY THOUGHTS

MY THOUGHTS

MY THOUGHTS

MY THOUGHTS

MY THOUGHTS

MY THOUGHTS

MY THOUGHTS

MY THOUGHTS

MY THOUGHTS

MY THOUGHTS

MY THOUGHTS

MY THOUGHTS

MY THOUGHTS

THINGS TO REMEMBER

Helpful resources and websites

- [ ] KinkInKolor.com
- [ ] Fetlife

MY OWN GLOSSARY
Write definitions of new terms, favorite words, or others to remember

MY OWN GLOSSARY
Write definitions of new terms, favorite words, or others to remember

My Reading List

TITLE	AUTHOR	RATING
		★★★★★
		★★★★★
		★★★★★
		★★★★★
		★★★★★
		★★★★★
		★★★★★
		★★★★★
		★★★★★
		★★★★★
		★★★★★
		★★★★★
		★★★★★

My Movie List

TITLE	RATING
	★★★★★
	★★★★★
	★★★★★
	★★★★★
	★★★★★
	★★★★★
	★★★★★
	★★★★★
	★★★★★
	★★★★★
	★★★★★
	★★★★★
	★★★★★

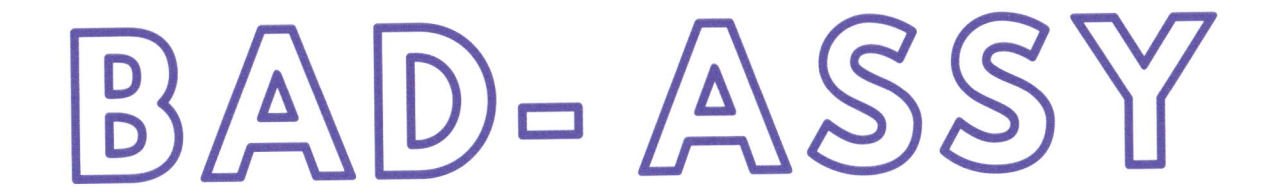

STAY CLASSY
Sassy
AND A BIT
BAD-ASSY

Made in the USA
Columbia, SC
20 March 2025